My b Book

by Jane Belk Moncure

illustrated by Linda Hohag

THE CHILD'S WORLD

ELGIN, ILLINOIS 60120

Library of Congress Cataloging in Publication Data

Moncure, Jane Belk.
  My "b" book.

  (My first steps to reading)
  Rev. ed. of: My b sound box. © 1977.
  Summary: Little b goes for a walk and finds many
things that begin with the letter "b" to put in her
box.
  1. Children's stories, American.   [1. Alphabet]
I. Hohag, Linda. ill.   II. Moncure, Jane Belk.   My
b sound box.   III. Title.   IV. Series: Moncure, Jane
Belk.   My first steps to reading.
PZ7.M739Myb   1984   [E]   84-17536
ISBN 0-89565-277-3

Distributed by Childrens Press, 1224 West Van Buren Street,
Chicago, Illinois 60607.

My "b" Book

(Blends are included in this book.)

Little **b** had a **box**.

6

"I will fill my **box**."

Little put on a bonnet.

She went for a walk.

Little  found a bird

and a birdbath.

She put them into her box.

Little **b** found a bunny.

Did she put the bunny into her box?

She did.

Little **b** found a bee.

She put the bee into her box.

Then she found a ...

baby   baboon...

and a big banana.

"In you go," said Little b.

The box was full.

Then she found a

bicycle

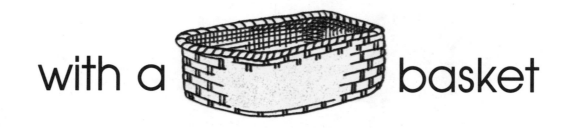

with a basket

on it.

She put her  into

the basket.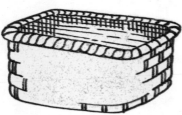

She rode away.

But the baby baboon, the bunny, the bird, and the box fell off the bicycle.

Little  fell off too.

"That was a bad bump," she said.

Then she
found a ball and
a bat.

"Let's play ball," she said.

The baby baboon
hit the ball.

A bear found it.

"Bear,"
said Little 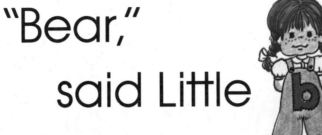.

"Give me
the ball."

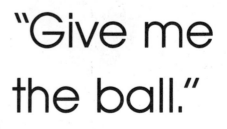

22

Then she put all her things into her box.

She put the bear in too.

23

"My box is too full.

It may break," said Little b .

24

She rode over
a bridge.

She found a big boat.

"The boat is just right for all my things," she said.

And it was!

More words with Little

balloon

barn

butterfly

bathtub

bell

bug

28

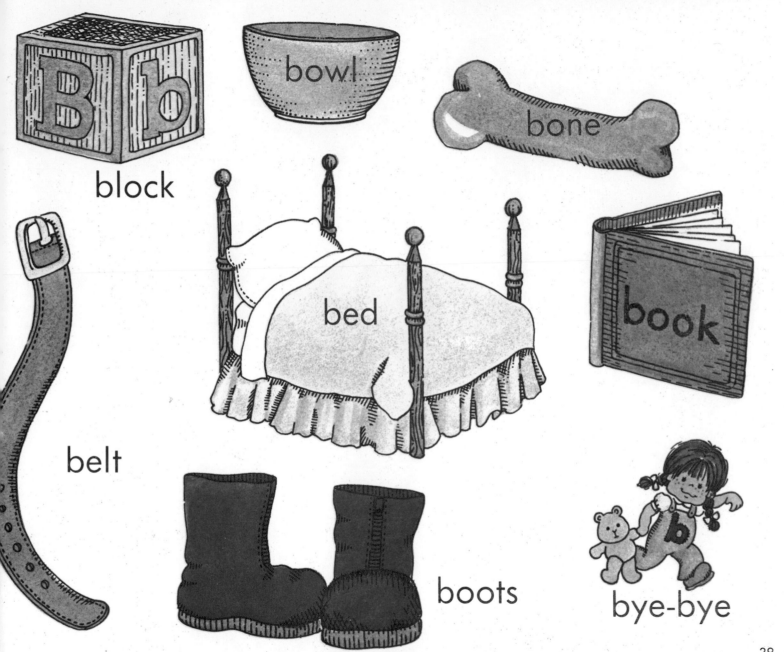

block

bowl

bone

belt

bed

book

boots

bye-bye

29